Nita Mehta's
51 Indian Recipes

Nita Mehta

B.Sc. (Home Science), M.Sc. (Food and Nutrition), Gold Medalist

SNAB
Excellence in Books

Nita Mehta's
51 Indian Recipes

© Copyright 2009 **SNAB** Publishers Pvt Ltd

First Edition 2009
ISBN 978-81-7869-278-4

Food Styling and Photography: **SNAB**

Layout and Laser Typesetting :

National Information
Technology Academy
3A/3, Asaf Ali Road
New Delhi-110002
☎ 23252948

Published by :

SNAB
Excellence in Books
Publishers Pvt. Ltd.
3A/3 Asaf Ali Road,
New Delhi - 110002
Tel: 23252948, 23250091
Telefax:91-11-23250091

Editorial and Marketing office:
E-159, Greater Kailash-II, N.Delhi-48
Fax: 91-11-29225218
Tel: 91-11-29214011
E-Mail: nitamehta@email.com
nitamehta@nitamehta.com
Website: http://www.nitamehta.com
Website: http://www.snabindia.com

Contributing Writers :
Anurag Mehta
Subhash Mehta

Editorial & Proofreading :
Rakesh
Ramesh

Distributed by :

THE VARIETY BOOK DEPOT
A.V.G. Bhavan, M 3 Con Circus,
New Delhi - 110 001
Tel : 23417175, 23412567; Fax : 23415335
Email: varietybookdepot@rediffmail.com

Printed by :
BATRA ART PRESS, NEW DELHI

Rs. 125/-

Introduction

The true art of Indian cooking lies in the subtle use and variation of spices which make each dish exotic and an exciting new experience. The use of spices, however, does not mean their use in vast amounts, nor does it mean that all Indian food is extremely hot and spicy, as many people believe. The dishes can be as hot or as mild as the individual family chooses, since this is a matter of personal taste. The best Indian dishes are a clever blend of exotic spices, delicate herbs with vegetables or meat. I have tried to make the recipes as simple as possible, giving step-by-step instructions, allowing you to enjoy the exotic flavour and aroma of Indian food, any time of the week.

Nita Mehta

WHAT'S IN A CUP?

INDIAN CUP
1 teacup = 200 ml liquid
AMERICAN CUP
1 cup = 240 ml liquid (8 oz.)
The recipes in this book were tested with the Indian teacup which holds 200 ml liquid.

Contents

RICE, PARANTHAS, RAITAS & ACHAARS 88

DESSERTS   116

Herbs & Spices

ENGLISH NAME	HINDI NAME	ENGLISH NAME	HINDI NAME
1 Asafoetida	1 Hing	18 Fenugreek Seeds	18 Methi Dana
2 Bay Leaves	2 Tej Patta	19 Fenugreek Leaves, Dried	19 Kasuri Methi
3 Cardamom, Green	3 Illaichi, Chhoti Illaichi	20 Garam Masala Powder	20 Garam Masala
4 Cardamom, Black	4 Moti Illaichi	21 Garlic	21 Lahsun
5 Carom Seeds	5 Ajwain	22 Ginger	22 Adrak
6 Chillies, Green	6 Hari Mirch	23 Mace	23 Javitri
7 Chillies, Dry Red	7 Sukhi Sabut Lal Mirch	24 Mango Powder, Dried	24 Amchur
8 Chilli Powder, Red	8 Lal Mirch Powder	25 Melon Seeds	25 Magaz
9 Cinnamon	9 Dalchini	26 Mint Leaves	26 Pudina
10 Cloves	10 Laung	27 Mustard Seeds	27 Rai, Sarson
11 Coriander Seeds	11 Sabut Dhania	28 Nigella, Onion Seeds	28 Kalaunji
12 Coriander Seeds, ground	12 Dhania Powder	29 Nutmeg	29 Jaiphal
13 Coriander Leaves	13 Hara Dhania	30 Pepper corns	30 Sabut Kali Mirch
14 Cumin Seeds	14 Jeera	31 Pomegranate Seeds, Dried	31 Anardana
15 Cumin Seeds, black	15 Shah Jeera	32 Sesame Seeds	32 Til
16 Curry Leaves	16 Kari Patta	33 Saffron	33 Kesar
17 Fennel Seeds	17 Saunf	34 Turmeric Powder	34 Haldi

Home Made Indian Spice Blends

To perk up the flavour of Indian dishes.

GARAM MASALA

Makes ¼ cup

5-6 sticks cinnamon (*dalchini*), each 2" long

15-20 black cardamom pods (*moti illaichi*)

¾ tbsp cloves (*laung*)

2 tbsp black pepper corns (*saboot kali mirch*)

2 tbsp cumin seeds (*jeera*), ½ flower of mace (*javitri*)

1. Remove seeds of black cardamom. Discard skin.

2. Roast all ingredients together in a non-stick pan or a *tawa* for 2 minutes on low heat, stirring constantly, till fragrant.

3. Remove from heat. Cool. Grind to a fine powder in a clean coffee or spice grinder. Store in a small jar with a tight fitting lid.

Chaat Masala

Makes ¾ cup

3 tbsp cumin seeds (*jeera*)
1 tbsp ground ginger (*sonth*)
2 tsp carom seeds (*ajwain*)
2 tsp raw mango powder (*amchoor*)
2 tbsp ground black salt (*kala namak*)
1 tsp salt, 1 tsp ground black pepper
½ tsp ground nutmeg (*jaiphal*)

1. Roast cumin in a small non-stick pan or *tawa* to a golden brown colour. Transfer to a bowl and set aside.

2. Roast carom seeds over moderate heat for about 2 minutes, till fragrant.

3. Grind roasted cumin and carom. Mix in the remaining ingredients.

4. Store in an airtight jar.

TANDOORI MASALA

Makes ½ cup

2 tbsp coriander seeds (*saboot dhania*)

2 tbsp cumin seeds (*jeera*)

1 tsp fenugreek seeds (*methi daana*)

1 tbsp black pepper corns (*saboot kali mirch*)

1 tbsp cloves (*laung*)

seeds of 8 black cardamom pods (*moti illaichi*)

1 tbsp dried fenugreek leaves (*kasoori methi*)

1 tbsp ground cinnamon (*dalchini*)

½ tbsp ground ginger (*sonth*), ½ tsp red chilli powder

1. In a non-stick pan, roast together — coriander seeds, cumin, fenugreek seeds, black pepper corns, cloves and black cardamom, on moderate heat for about 1 minute, until fragrant.

2. Remove from heat and let the spices cool down. Grind to a fine powder. Transfer to a bowl and mix in the remaining ingredients. Store in an air tight jar.

Sambhar Powder

Makes ½ cup

¼ cup coriander seeds *(saboot dhania)*

1 tbsp cumin seeds *(jeera)*

1 tbsp, gram lentils *(channe ki dal)*

2 tsp fenugreek seeds *(methi daana)*

5-6 dry, red chillies *(saboot lal mirch)*

½ tsp asafoetida *(hing)*

1½ tsp pepper corns *(saboot kali mirch)*

1. Roast all ingredients together over low heat in a non-stick pan or a *tawa*, until fragrant.

2. Cool the spices and grind to a fine powder in a small coffee grinder. Store in an air tight jar.

The Indian Spice Box

Almost every Indian kitchen has this box with various compartments to hold the basic spices & salt.

Coriander Powder (*dhania powder*) — Cumin (*jeera*)

Salt — Turmeric (*haldi*)

Dry Mango Powder (*amchoor*) — Red Chilli Powder

Garam Masala

Some Cooking Utensils

Kadhai (wok) — The *kadhai* is a deep pan, round bottomed with two handles on the sides. Used mainly for frying and making Indian masala dishes. When buying one, choose a heavy bottomed one in a medium size. Steel/Brass *kadhai*s were used earlier, but now aluminium or non-stick ones are more popular. Copper-bottomed metal *kadhai*s are also becoming popular.

Tawa (griddle) — A heavy iron *tawa* makes good chappatis. Buy one with a handle. These days non stick griddles are also available.

Sauce Pan — These are deep pans with a handle. Useful for making tea, blanching vegetables in water or working with food where some sauce is needed. Usually these are made of stainless steel & are available in various sizes. Nonstick ones are also available.

Patila (*deep metal pans*) — Used for boiling water, milk, rice, pasta etc. Buy a heavy-bottom one. Deep non-stick pots with handles are also available which are very handy for making soups, rice and curries.

Non Stick Frying Pan (*saute pan, skillet*) — A pan about 2" high is ideal for shallow frying tikkis, kebabs and other snacks. It makes a good utensil for cooking dry/semi dry dishes too. The vegetables lie flat in a single layer on the wide bottom making them crunchy on the outside and yet moist from inside. Remember to use a plastic or a wooden spoon/spatula to stir and fry in all nonstick vessels. Metallic ones will scratch the non stick finish and ruin it. Avoid strong detergents for washing them, warm soapy water is best. It is good to have one small (about 7" diameter) and one big (10" diameter) pan. Dosas and pancakes too can be made conveniently in them.

Kadcchi (*laddle*) — Large, long - handled spoon with a small shallow bowl like spoon at the end. Should be strong enough for stirring masalas.

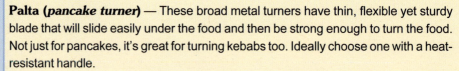

Palta (*pancake turner*) — These broad metal turners have thin, flexible yet sturdy blade that will slide easily under the food and then be strong enough to turn the food. Not just for pancakes, it's great for turning kebabs too. Ideally choose one with a heat-resistant handle.

Chakla-Belan (*rolling board-rolling pin*) — A marble or heavy weight rolling board is ideal for rolling out dough for chapatis, poori etc. A wooden rolling pin with it makes the set complete. Plastic rolling pins are available but I am not too comfortable with them.

Parat (*shallow bowl to knead dough*) — Shallow bowl to make dough, generally stainless steel. Buy a medium size even if you are a small family, because if the bowl is too small, the surrounding area tends to get messy while making the dough. Dough can also be made in a food processor.

Chhanni (*large steel colander*) — A big, wide strainer with large holes for draining cooked rice, pasta and for draining fresh vegetables after washing.

Chhara, Pauni (*slotted spoon*) — A big round, flat spoon with holes and a long handle. Good for removing fried food from oil as it drains out the oil nicely through the holes. Also used to lift solid foods out of cooking liquids.

Snacks

Moong Dal Tilli Pakore

In this speciality from Delhi, paneer cubes, tomatoes and capsicums are skewered on toothpicks (tilli), and dipped in a thick batter made from moong dal to give a crusty coating when deep-fried – no wonder they are so famous!.

Makes 24 pieces

200 gm cottage cheese (*paneer*) - cut into ¾" squares, of ¼-½" thickness

1 large capsicum - cut into ¾" pieces

2 tomatoes - cut into 4 pieces lengthwise, pulp removed and cut into ¾" pieces

some chaat masala, 24 toothpicks

BATTER

½ cup dehusked moong beans (*dhuli moong dal*) - soaked for 1-2 hours, 2 tbsp cornflour

2 tbsp fresh coriander (*hara dhania*) - chopped very finely, 1 green chilli - chopped very finely

½ tsp salt, or to taste, ½ tsp red chilli powder, 1 tsp coriander (*dhania*) powder

¼ tsp dried mango powder (*amchoor*), ½ tsp *garam masala*, 1-2 pinches of tandoori red colour (optional)

1. Soak dal for 1-2 hours. Strain. Grind in a mixer with little water to a smooth thick paste. Put in a bowl. Beat well by hand to make it light.

2. Add cornflour, coriander, green chilli, salt, red chilli powder, coriander powder, *amchoor* powder and *garam masala* to dal paste. Add colour. Add a little water to get a coating consistency. Keep aside.

3. Thread a capsicum, then a *paneer* and then a tomato piece on each tooth pick. Keep them spaced out on the stick. Keep aside till serving time.

4. To serve, heat oil for deep frying. Dip the *paneer* sticks in the prepared dal batter. Shake off the excess batter.

5. Deep fry 6-8 sticks at a time till golden. Serve hot sprinkled generously with *chaat masala*.

Galouti Kebab

PRESSURE COOK TOGETHER

500 gm lamb mince (*keema*)

¼ tsp nutmeg (*jaiphal*) powder, ¼ tsp mace (*javetri*)

seeds of 3 black cardamoms (*moti illaichi*), 2" stick cinnamon (*dalchini*)

OTHER INGREDIENTS

¼ tsp soda-bi-carb (*mitha soda*), 2 tbsp oil

2 onions - cut into slices, 2 tbsp ginger-garlic paste

1 egg white - separate egg yolk from egg white, 4 tbsp gram flour (*besan*), 2 tbsp chopped coriander

1 tsp *tandoori masala*, ½ tsp *garam masala*, ½ tsp red chilli powder, 1¼ tsp salt

3 tbsp butter

oil for frying

1. Wash the mince in a strainer and press out excess water. Put the mince in a cooker. Add ¼ tsp nutmeg, ¼ tsp mace, seeds of 3 black cardamoms, 1" stick cinnamon and ½ cup water. Give 5-6 whistles. Remove from fire. The *keema* should be cooked. After the pressure drops, if there is any water, dry out the water completely on fire. Let it cool.

2. Place boiled mince in a mixer blender. Churn till smooth. Keep aside.

3. Heat 1 cup oil in a *kadhai* and fry the sliced onions till golden brown. Remove from oil with a slotted spoon and grind to a brown paste.

4. Add the brown onion paste, ginger-garlic paste, soda-bi-carb, oil, 1 egg white, salt, chilli powder, *tandoori masala* and *garam masala* to mince. Mix to get a sticky consistency. Remove to a bowl.

5. Roast gram flour in a *kadhai* or pan on low heat till light golden and fragrant.

6. Add roasted gram flour and chopped coriander to the mince mixture. Add butter. Keep for 1 hour in the refrigerator. Shape mince into flat, 4" diameter tikkis.

7. Shallow fry on low heat in 1-2 tbsp oil on a *tawa* or pan, till brown on both sides. Sprinkle some *chaat masala* and serve with onion rings mixed with some lemon juice and dahi pudina chutney. Serve hot.

Dahi Kebab

Hung yogurt is thickened with roasted gram flour (besan) and shaped into incredibly light kebabs – these are carefully coated with golden fried onions dissolved in milk!

Serves 4-5

2 cups yogurt (*dahi*) - hang in a muslin cloth for
3-4 hours to drain off liquid completely

½ cup gram flour (*besan*)

2 tsp garlic paste, 1 onion - cut into thin slices

¼ cup milk to sprinkle, ¾ cup oil to shallow fry

DAHI KEBAB MASALA

seeds of 4 green cardamoms (*chhoti illaichi*)

½" stick cinnamon (*dalchini*), 8-10 cloves (*laung*)

½ tsp black pepper (*kali mirch*)

1 tsp salt, 1½-2 tsp red chilli powder

1. Roast gram flour for about 2 minutes till it changes colour and turns light golden. Sift the besan to make it smooth and light. Keep aside.

2. Heat oil in a frying pan. Fry sliced onions till golden brown, remove and grind to a paste. Keep fried onion paste aside till serving time.

3. Crush cardamom, cinnamon and cloves for *dahi kebab masala*. Add salt, pepper and red chilli to it. Keep masala powder aside.

4. Mix 2 tsp of the above masala powder to the hung yogurt, keeping the remaining masala powder for use in step 6. Add garlic and besan also and mix well. Divide into 20 equal parts. Flatten, wetting hands with a little water to give the kebabs smooth and even shape. Chill in the fridge for at least 30 minutes.

5. Heat the oil in the pan and fry the kebabs on low heat, turning after a minute to brown both sides. Keep aside till serving time.

6. To serve, put fried onion paste in the pan on low heat. Add the remaining masala powder, stir and add the fried kebabs. Gently mix. Sprinkle milk on the kebabs, turn side and sprinkle milk on the other side too. Remove and serve at once.

Tandoori Bharwaan Aloo

3 big (longish) potatoes, some *chaat masala* to sprinkle

FILLING

3 almonds (*badaam*) - crushed roughly with a rolling pin (*belan*), 1 tbsp mint leaves - chopped

1 green chilli - remove seeds and chop, 4 tbsp grated *paneer,* ¼ tsp salt or to taste

¼ tsp garam masala, ¼ tsp red chilli powder, a pinch dried mango powder (*amchoor*)

COVERING

½ cup thick curd (*dahi*) - hang in a muslin cloth for 30 minutes, 1 tbsp ginger paste

¼ tsp red chilli powder, ¾ tsp salt, ¼ tsp red or orange tandoori colour or turmeric (*haldi*)

BHARWAAN ALOO MASALA

1 tsp black cumin (*shah jeera*), seeds of 2 brown cardamoms (*moti illaichi*)

6-8 pepper corns (*saboot kali mirch*), 2-3 blades of mace (*javetri*)

1. Boil potatoes in salted water till just tender. When they are no longer hot, peel skin.

2. For the filling, mix crushed almonds with mint leaves, green chillies, grated *paneer*, salt, *garam masala*, red chilli and *amchoor*.

3. Grind or crush cumin seeds, seeds of black cardamom, pepper corns and 2-3 pinches of mace to a coarse powder.

4. To the *paneer* filling, add ¼-½ tsp of the above freshly ground masala powder also. Keep the leftover powder aside.

5. For the covering, mix hung curd, ginger paste, remaining freshly ground masala powder, red chilli and salt. Add turmeric or orange colour.

6. Run the tip of a fork on the back surface of the potatoes, making the surface rough. (The rough surface holds the curd well). Cut each potato into 2 halves. Scoop out, just a little, to get a small cavity in each potato with the back of a teaspoon. Stuff with *paneer* filling.

7. With a spoon apply the curd on the back and sides of the potato. Grill potatoes in a gas tandoor or a preheated oven for 15 minutes on a greased wire rack till they get slightly dry.

8. Spoon some oil or melted butter on them (baste) and then grill further till the coating turns absolutely dry. Sprinkle some chaat masala and serve hot.

Seekh Lahori

Recapture the taste of a night in the crowded bazaars of old Lahore with this authentic but easy recipe.

Serves 6

800 gm mutton mince (*keema*)

1 onion - finely chopped, 1½" piece of ginger - finely chopped, 8 flakes of garlic - finely chopped

4 green chillies - deseeded & finely chopped, 3 tbsp chopped coriander (*hara dhania*)

2 eggs, 4 tbsp grated cheddar cheese

1 tbsp chopped mint (*pudina*), 2 tbsp roasted gram flour (*besan*)

LAHORI SEEKH MASALA

1 tsp pomegranate seeds (*anaar daana*), 1 tsp black pepper corns (*saboot kali mirch*)

seeds of 2 green cardamoms (*chhoti illaichi*), seeds of 1 black cardamom (*moti illaichi*)

1" stick cinnamon (*dalchini*), 2 cloves (*laung*), a pinch of nutmeg (*jaiphal*), ¾ tsp rock salt (*kala namak*)

BASTING

desi ghee or melted butter for basting

1. Wash the mince (*keema*) in a strainer and gently press to squeeze out all the water. Grind in a grinder to make it fine and sticky. Mash well with the heel of your palm.

2. Powder all ingredients for *lahori seekh masala* together in a small grinder.

3. In a large flat vessel (*parat*) add mince, onion, ginger, garlic, green chillies, coriander, eggs, cheese, mint, gram flour and the ground spices. Mix well with the help of your palm. Divide into 16-18 balls and keep aside for 2 hours.

4. Heat an oven with greased skewers at 180°C. Cover the wire rack of the oven with foil. Grease the foil well with oil.

5. Take one ball of the mince mixture at a time and hold a hot skewer carefully in the other hand. Carefully press the mince on to the hot skewer. The mince will immediately stick to the skewer.

6. Make another seekh on the same skewer, leaving a gap of 2". Repeat with the left over mince on all the other skewers.

7. Place the skewers on the wire rack with foil. Put in the oven. Cook for 10-15 minutes, change sides, baste with ghee or melted butter. Cook for another 5 minutes. When cooked, gently remove the kebab from the skewers with the help of a cloth. Serve cut into 2" pieces with mint chutney.

Shami Kebab

Makes 15 kebabs

PRESSURE COOK TOGETHER

½ kg mutton mince (*keema*)

¼ cup *channa dal* - soaked in warm water for 20-30 minutes and drained

1 onion - sliced, 10 flakes garlic - chopped

2" piece ginger - chopped

2 tsp coriander seeds (*saboot dhania*)

1 tsp cumin (*jeera*), 3-4 cloves (*laung*)

2 green cardamoms (*chhoti illaichi*), 2 black cardamoms (*moti illaichi*) - opened

½" stick cinnamon (*dalchini*), 1 bay leaves (*tej patta*)

4-5 pepper corns (*saboot kali mirch*), 2-3 dry, whole red chillies

½ cup water

1 tsp salt, or to taste

1. Wash mince in a strainer and press well to drain out water. Add mince and all the remaining ingredients in a pressure cooker. Pressure cook to give 2 whistles. Keep on low flame for 2 minutes. Remove from fire.

2. When the pressure drops, uncover the pressure cooker. If there is any water left, keep the cooker on fire to dry the water. (If the mince is wet, the kebabs will break while frying).

3. Remove skin of black cardamom. Grind the well dried mince in a mixer till smooth.

4. Make balls. Flatten them to get thick, round 2½" diameter tikkis.

5. Shallow fry in a 2 tbsp oil in a pan on medium heat, till brown. Serve.

Amritsari Fish

The beauty of these golden, batter-fried fingers is that the delicate taste and texture of fish (preferably sole) is not overwhelmed with spices – just one shining accent note of ajwain (carom seeds).

Serves 5-6

500 gm boneless fish fillet - cut into 1½" long pieces (10-12 pieces)

¼ tsp turmeric (*haldi*) powder, 1 tsp salt, 1 tbsp lemon juice, 2 tbsp gram flour (*besan*)

BATTER

3 tbsp flour (*maida*), 4 tbsp cornflour, 3 tbsp gram flour (*besan*), 1 egg

1 tsp carom seeds (*ajwain*), 2 tsp garlic paste

2 tsp ginger paste, ¾ tsp salt

1½ tsp red chilli powder, 1 tbsp lemon juice

a pinch of colour; ¼ cup water, approx.

TO SERVE

some chaat masala for sprinkling on top, hari chutney, one large lemon - cut into wedges

1. Cut fish into 1½" long pieces of ¼" thickness.

2. Rub fish pieces with turmeric, salt, lemon juice and gram flour. Keep aside for 20 minutes. Wash well to remove all smell. Pat dry on a clean kitchen towel.

3. Mix together all ingredients of the batter to get a pouring batter of thin coating consistency.

4. Leave the fish to marinate in it for at least 2 hours or till serving time in the fridge.

5. At the time of serving, heat oil on medium heat. Pick up the fish pieces, deep fry to a golden colour on low medium heat till the fish is cooked and crisp.

6. Sprinkle *chaat masala* and serve hot garnished with lemon wedges and sprigs of coriander or mint.

Note: For a different flavour 1-1½ tsp dry fenugreek leaves (*kasoori methi*) can be added to the batter.

Peshawari Seekh

Makes 12

1½ cup soya granules (nutri nugget granules)

100 gm *paneer* - grated (1 cup)

1" piece ginger - chopped (1 tbsp)

2 green chillies - finely chopped

4 tbsp green coriander (*hara dhania*) - chopped

seeds of 4 green cardamoms (*chhoti illaich i*) - crushed or 2-3 drops kewra essence

¼ tsp mace (*javitri*) powder, optional

1 tsp channa masala

1 tsp salt, ½ tsp red chilli powder

2 bread slices - broken into pieces and churned in a mixer to get fresh crumbs

1. Soak soya granules in 1 cup of hot water for 15 minutes.

2. Strain. Squeeze out the water well from the soya granules. (No water should remain). You can also put the soya granules in a muslin cloth and squeeze.

3. Add grated *paneer*, ginger, green chillies, coriander, cardamoms, mace powder, *channa masala*, salt, and red chilli powder.

4. Churn the nutri granules along with all the other ingredients in a mixer till smooth.

5. Churn bread in a grinder, to get fresh bread crumbs. Add fresh crumbs to the nutri nuggets mixture. Mix well.

6. Divide the mixture into 12 equal portions and make balls.

7. Take a ball of nutri mixture and make a 2" long kebab.

8. Take a pencil or a skewer and push it carefully from one end of kebab to the other, without puncturing at any point.

9. Gently pull out skewer or the pencil. Keep the seekhs in the fridge for ½ hour.

10. Deep fry the seekhs in medium hot oil in a *kadhai* to a light brown colour. Serve hot with chutney.

Paalak Pakoras

Pakoras – deep-fried vegetable fritters made with a gram flour batter – have many variations. In this recipe, batter-coated spinach leaves make a crisp and delicious snack to serve at any time of the day.

Serves 4-5

24 spinach (*paalak*) leaves with 2" long stems

BATTER

½ cup gram flour (*besan*)

¼ cup semolina (*suji*)

½ tsp carom seeds (*ajwain*)

½ tsp salt, ¼ tsp red chilli powder

½ tsp coriander (*dhania*) powder

¾ cup water or as required

oil to deep-fry

1. Take spinach leaves including a little stem of about 2". Wash the spinach and pat dry on a clean kitchen towel.

2. Put all the ingredients for the batter in a bowl, adding water to make a thick batter with a coating consistency. Do not make it thin as it will not coat the leaves properly.

3. Heat the oil in a wok.

4. Dip each spinach leaf in batter so that it gets well coated.

5. Fry the leaves on medium heat, a few at a time, till golden and crisp on both sides. Remove and drain on absorbent paper towels. Serve immediately.

Jhinga Til Tinka

A sensuous experience! Bite into a sesame-flavoured crumbly coating; then go to deeper layers of textured and creamy secrets, scented with subtle spices.

Makes 16

500 gm medium sized prawns - cleaned and deveined, juice of ½ lemon, oil for deep fry

1ST MARINADE

5 tsp garlic paste (16-18 flakes of garlic), 4 tsp ginger paste (2" piece of ginger)

½ tsp white or black pepper powder, ½ tsp red chilli powder, ¼ tsp salt, 4 tbsp lemon juice

2ND MARINADE

½ cup yogurt (*dahi*), ¼ cup cream, ½ tsp salt, a pinch of tandoori colour, ½ cup grated cheddar cheese

1½ tsp carom seeds (*ajwain*), ½ tsp green cardamom (*chhoti illaichi*) powder, 3 tbsp gram flour (*besan*)

COATING

2 tbsp black sesame seeds (*til*)

1 cup fresh bread-crumbs (grind 2 bread slices in a blender to get fresh crumbs)

1. Sprinkle ½ tsp salt and juice of ½ lemon. Mix and keep aside for 15 minutes. Wash well and pat dry.

2. Mix all the ingredients of the 1st marinade in a bowl. Add prawns and mix gently. Keep aside for 30 minutes.

3. Mix all ingredients of the 2nd marinade in another bowl. Mix well. Add prawns with the 1st marinade to the 2nd marinade in the bowl. Keep aside for 30 minutes.

4. Skewer one prawn on each wooden stick or big toothpicks.

5. Mix bread-crumbs with sesame seeds, roll the skewered prawns in the coating mixture and refrigerate for 15 minutes.

6. Heat oil in a *kadhai* and deep fry 1-2 pieces at a time over medium heat for 2-3 minutes. Serve with pudina chutney.

Mughlai Malai Tikka

Soak chicken cubes in a classic cream marinade – grill while basting with butter to make moist mouth-watering morsels. Be sure to make a large quantity to serve as appetizers to young men who have their drinks in hand!

Serves 6-7

500 gm boneless chicken - cut into 1½" pieces

MARINADE

½ cup thick cream, 4 tbsp grated cheese, 4 tbsp cashewnuts (*kaju*), 1 egg white

¼ tsp green cardamom powder (seeds of 2-3 *chhoti illaichi* - crushed), 1 tsp white or black pepper powder

1 tsp garlic paste, 2 tsp ginger paste, 1 tbsp cornflour, 1 tbsp butter or ghee

½ tsp garam masala powder, ¼ tsp dried mango powder (*amchoor*)

½ tsp cumin seeds (*jeera*) powder, 1½ tsp salt, 1 green chilli - crushed, optional

BASTING

2 tbsp melted butter or oil

1. Soak cashewnuts for 15 minutes in hot water. Drain and grind to a paste.

2. Mash cheese in a big vessel (*parat*). Add cream and egg. Mix well.

3. Mix all the ingredients of the marinade — green cardamom powder, white pepper, ginger-garlic paste, cornflour, butter, *garam masala*, *amchoor*, cumin powder, salt and green chillies.

4. Marinate chicken covered with a plastic wrap/cling film for 2 hours or till serving time in the refrigerator.

5. Heat an oven at 180°C or heat a gas tandoor on gas for 15 minutes on low heat. Cover the wire rack with aluminium foil. Grease foil with oil.

6. Place the well coated chicken pieces on the greased grill or skewer the chicken pieces. Roast for 10 minutes or until cooked, thoroughly basting (brushing) with melted butter or oil at least once in between. Roast for another 5 minutes.

7. Sprinkle *chaat masala* and serve hot with pudina chutney.

Paneer Pasanda Tikka

300 gm whole block of cottage cheese (*paneer*) - cut into ½" thick slices, some chaat masala

MARINADE (MIX TOGETHER)

1 cup curd (*dahi*) - hang in a muslin cloth for 30 minutes

8-10 flakes of garlic, 1" piece ginger, 2 dry, red chillies - all ground together to a paste

1 tbsp oil, 1½ tsp channa masala, ¾ tsp salt or to taste

1 tsp dry fenugreek leaves (*kasoori methi*), 1 tsp lemon juice, 2-3 tbsp thick cream

FILLING

½ tsp cumin seeds (*jeera*), ¼ cup very finely chopped onion, ¼ cup very finely chopped cabbage

1 small carrot - grated finely & squeezed, ½ of a small capsicum - very finely chopped (¼ cup)

4-5 cashewnuts (*kaju*) - chopped finely, 1 tsp raisins (*kishmish*) - chopped

2 tbsp finely chopped coriander (*hara dhania*)

½ tsp salt or to taste, ½ tsp chaat masala, ¼ tsp turmeric (*haldi*)

1. Sprinkle *chaat masala* on both sides of *paneer* slices. Keep aside.

2. Heat 1 tbsp oil in a non-stick pan or a *tawa*. Remove pan from fire and swirl or rotate it to coat the bottom with oil. Put the *paneer* slices on the hot pan and saute them till golden brown on both sides. Remove from pan and cut each lengthwise into half carefully, to get 2 slices from each piece. Keep aside.

3. For filling, heat 1 tbsp oil, add cumin. Stir for a few seconds. Add onion. Cook till soft. Add cabbage, carrot, capsicum, cashews and raisins. Saute for 2 minutes.

4. Add coriander, salt, *chaat masala* and turmeric. Cook for a minute. Remove from fire.

5. Mix all ingredients of the marinade in a big shallow dish. Place a piece of cottage cheese on a flat surface or plate. Spread some marinade on one side of the *paneer*.

6. Sprinkle the cooked vegetable on the same side of the slice. Cover slice completely with the filling. Place the other piece of *paneer* on the first piece, keeping the brown side on top. Press the sandwiched *paneer* nicely.

7. Put the sandwiched *paneer* in the marinade in the bowl and turn side to cover completely with the marinade on all the sides. To serve, grill for 10-15 minutes till coating turns dry. Cut each from the middle into 2 pieces. Sprinkle *chaat masala*.

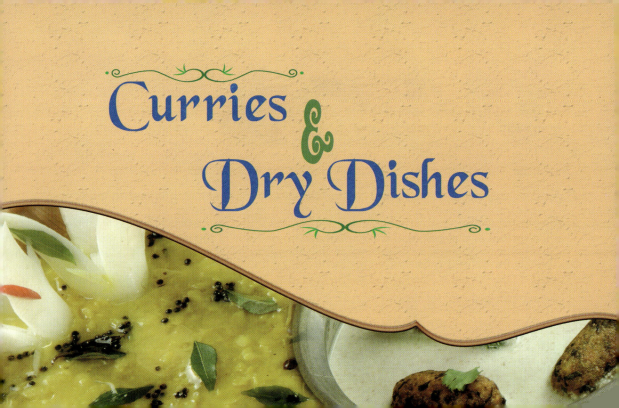

Curries & Dry Dishes

Quick Butter Chicken

Marinated chicken is cooked till tender, then simmered in a rich gravy made from pureed tomatoes, butter, cream and cashew paste. Degi mirch gives a beautiful red colour, enhancing the appetizing look.

Serves 4

1 medium sized chicken (800 gm) - cut into 12 pieces, 6 tbsp oil

MARINADE

1 tbsp garlic paste, 1 tsp ginger paste, 1 tsp *garam masala*, few drops of orange red colour

1 tbsp dry fenugreek leaves (*kasoori methi*), ½ tsp black salt (*kala namak*), ¾ tsp salt

MAKHANI GRAVY

½ kg (6-7) tomatoes or 2 cups ready-made tomato puree, 2 tbsp butter, 2-3 tbsp oil

1 bay leaf (*tej patta*), 4 tbsp cashewnuts (*kaju*)

2 tbsp ginger-garlic paste or 1" piece of ginger & 16-18 flakes of garlic - crushed to a paste

¾ tsp *kashmiri laal mirch* or *degi mirch*, 1 cup milk, 2 tbsp cream, ½ tsp *garam masala*

1 tsp salt, or to taste, 1 tsp *tandoori masala* (optional), ¼ tsp sugar or to taste

1. Soak cashewnuts in hot water for 15 minutes, drain and grind to a very fine paste with a little water in a mixer.

2. Wash the chicken well. Pat dry chicken with a clean kitchen napkin.

3. For the marinade, mix garlic and ginger paste, dry fenugreek leaves, black salt, salt, *garam masala* and colour. Rub the chicken with this mixture. Keep aside for 15 minutes.

4. Heat 6 tbsp oil in a *kadhai*, add marinated chicken, cook on high heat for 7-8 minutes, stirring all the time. Reduce heat and cook covered for 10-15 minutes or till tender. Remove from fire. Keep aside.

5. To prepare the makhani gravy, boil water in a pan. Add tomatoes to boiling water. Boil for 3-4 minutes. Remove from water and peel. Let it cool down. Grind blanched tomatoes to a smooth puree. Keep aside.

6. Heat butter and oil together in a *kadhai*. Add tej patta. Stir for a few seconds. Add ginger and garlic paste, cook until liquid evaporates and the paste just changes colour.

7. Add pureed tomatoes or ready-made puree, *degi mirch* and sugar. Cook until the puree turns very dry and oil starts to float on top.

8. Add prepared cashew paste, stir for a few seconds on medium heat till fat separates. Lower the heat. Add about 1 cup of water to get the desired gravy. Add salt. Bring to a boil, stirring constantly.

9. Add cooked chicken. Cover and simmer for 5-7 minutes till the gravy turns to a bright colour. Reduce heat. Add milk on very low heat and bring to a boil, stirring continuously. Keep stirring for 1-2 minutes on low heat till you get the desired thickness of the gravy.

10. Remove from fire and stir in cream, stirring continuously. Add *garam masala* and *tandoori masala*. Stir. Garnish with 1 tbsp of fresh cream, slit green chillies and coriander. Serve hot with nan.

Rogan Josh

The best of Kashmiri cuisine: this curry has a thin and delicate gravy with the traditional taste created by the use of fennel and dry ginger.

Serves 4

½ kg lamb (*mutton*)

½ cup thick yogurt (*dahi*)

¼ tsp asafoetida (*hing*) powder

6 tbsp oil

½ tsp red chilli powder (*degi mirch*)

salt to taste

GRIND TOGETHER & SIEVE TO GET A FINE POWDER

1 tbsp ginger powder (*saunth*), 2 tsp fennel (*saunf*)

3-4 cloves (*laung*), seeds of 3 brown cardamoms (*moti illaich i*)

2 tsp cumin seeds (*jeera*), 3-4 dry, red chillies

1. Wash and pat dry mutton on a kitchen towel.

2. Heat oil in a pressure cooker. Add hing.

3. Add dry meat and stir fry for 4-5 minutes or till the mutton turns dry, golden brown and gives a well fried look. There should be no water of the meat left.

4. Add degi mirch. Mix well.

5. Mix the curd with the sifted powdered masala. Add this curd to the mutton. Add salt. Stir fry for 5-7 minutes till the curd blends well and turns dry.

6. Add 2 cups of water, pressure cook for 7 minutes on full flame. Reduce flame and cook for 5 minutes. Remove from fire and let the pressure drop by itself. Check for tenderness. Serve hot with rice or roti.

Lucknawi Koftas

These potato and spinach koftas are simmered in delicate gravy enriched with almonds, melon seeds and poppy seeds – a marvel of tastes and aromas.

Serves 4

KOFTAS

125 gm potatoes - boiled and mashed, ¼ cup chopped coriander (*hara dhania*)

¼ cup cornflour, ½ cup chopped spinach (*paalak*)

2 tbsp dry fenugreek leaves (*kasoori methi*), ½ tsp garam masala, 1 tbsp lemon juice

1 tsp salt, or to taste, oil for deep frying

MASALA PASTE

12 almonds (*badaam*), 4 tbsp melon seeds (*magaz*), 6 green chillies

4 tbsp poppy seeds (*khus khus*), 1 onion, ½" piece of ginger, 3-4 flakes of garlic

OTHER INGREDIENTS

3 tbsp oil, 2 onions - finely chopped cup yogurt (*dahi*)

½ cup milk, ¼ cup cream, ½ tsp turmeric (*haldi*), ½ cup water, 1 tsp sugar, 1 tsp salt

1. Mix all ingredients of the koftas together in a bowl. Form into 1½" long rolls and deep fry 1-2 at a time in hot oil and keep aside.

2. Grind all ingredients for the masala paste together in a mixer to a fine paste.

3. For the gravy, heat 3 tbsp oil add chopped onions, stir till golden brown.

4. Add the ground masala paste & fry for a 2-3 minutes.

5. Reduce heat, stirring continuously add yogurt, milk, cream, turmeric, sugar and salt. Increase heat bring to a boil, stirring continuously.

6. Add ½ cup water and cook for another 5 minutes. Remove from fire and keep aside till serving time.

7. At the time of serving heat up the gravy add the koftas and simmer for a minute for the koftas to get hot. Serve hot.

Rajasthani Gatte ki Subzi

A dough made of gram flour is used to make the steamed gatte. The curry has a base of curd, gram flour and pureed tomatoes – spicy, chilli hot and brightly coloured like the place of its origin.

Serves 4-5

GATTE

¾ cup gram flour (*besan*), ¼ tsp baking soda (*mitha soda*), ½ tsp ginger-green chilli paste

¼ tsp carom seeds (*ajwain*), ¼ tsp fennel (*saunf*) - crushed, ½ tsp salt, ½ tsp turmeric (*haldi*)

½ tsp red chilli powder, ½ tsp coriander (*dhania*) powder, ½ tsp garam masala, 2 tbsp yogurt, 1 tbsp oil

CURRY

2 tbsp oil, 2 cloves (*laung*), 1 tsp cumin seeds (*jeera*), 1 cardamom (*moti illaichi*) - crushed

¼ tsp turmeric (*haldi*), ½ tsp red chilli powder, 2 tomatoes - puree in a mixer & strain, ½ tsp ginger paste

1 green chilli - crushed, 1 cup yogurt (*dahi*) mixed with 2 tsp gram flour (*besan*) & 1 cup water till smooth

1. Sift besan and soda. Add ginger chilli paste, carom seeds, fennel, powdered spices and just enough curd to get a very soft dough. Mix well. Mix 1 tbsp oil and knead again. Make 4 balls. With the help of oil smeared on your hands, roll out thin fingers 3"-4" long, like cylinders.

2. Boil 5 cups of water. Keep the gatte in a stainless steel round strainer and keep the strainer on the pan of boiling water and cover with a lid.

3. Steam gatte for 5-7 minutes. Let them cool. Later cut them into rounds of ½" thickness. Keep aside.

4. For curry, blend curd, gram flour and 1 cup water in a mixer till very smooth. Puree tomatoes and strain them to get a smooth puree.

5. Heat 2 tbsp oil, add cloves, cumin, cardamom, turmeric and red chilli powder. Stir.

6. Add tomato puree, ginger and crushed chilli. Cook for 3 minutes till dry and oil separates.

7. Reduce heat. Add curd with gram flour. Stir constantly, on low heat to bring it to a boil. Simmer for 3-4 minutes.

8. Add gatte. Cook for 2-3 minutes. Serve hot garnished with green coriander.

Kerala Chicken Stew

The cuisine of Kerala reflects the beauty of the land – this boneless chicken stew has a sweetly delicious coconut gravy choc-a-bloc with fresh, colourful vegetables.

Serves 6

250 gm boneless chicken - cut into 2" square pieces

2 cups of any combination of sliced mixed vegetables - (mushrooms, baby corn, snow peas French beans, cauliflower, carrots, potatoes and onion)

4 tsp oil

seeds of 6-8 green cardamoms (*chhoti illaich i*), 2½" stick of cinnamon (*dalchini*), 6-8 cloves (*laung*)

1 green chilli - deseeded & cut into half, 2½" piece of ginger - thinly sliced, 10-12 curry leaves

2 cups coconut milk, 1 tsp salt

1 tsp black pepper corns (*saboot kali mirch*) - coarsely ground

1. Heat oil in a pan, add seeds of green cardamom, cinnamon and cloves. Wait for a minute. Add green chilli, ginger and curry patta. Saute for 2 minutes.

2. Add potatoes, carrots and onions. Cover and cook for 4 minutes.

3. Add the remaining vegetables, then add the chicken and stir-fry for 4-5 minutes.

4. Lower the heat, add the coconut milk and 1½ cups of water. Simmer for 8-10 minutes or until the chicken is cooked and the gravy thickens.

5. Remove from the heat. Add salt and stir well.

6. Sprinkle with black pepper and serve with Appams or boiled rice.

Tips: 1. Always simmer the coconut milk on a very low heat without covering, to prevent from curdling.

      2. Add the salt to the coconut milk right in the end, after it has been boiled to prevent from curdling.

Goan Fish Curry

Another landscape, another cuisine – this curry has tamarind and coconut milk,
curry leaves and black mustard seeds.

Serves 4

400 gm of any firm white fish - cut into 2" pieces

4 tbsp oil

2-3 green chillies - deseeded and sliced, 1 tsp red chilli powder

2 tsp coriander (*dhania*) powder, ½ tsp garam masala, 1 tsp salt

2 cups thick coconut milk, 2 tbsp tamarind (*imli*) pulp, optional, 1 cup water

PASTE

1 medium onion, 2½" piece of ginger, 8-10 flakes of garlic

TEMPERING (*TADKA*)

2 tbsp oil, 1 tsp black mustard seeds (*sarson*)

8-10 curry leaves (*curry patta*), 3 whole dry red chillies

1. Make a paste of onion, ginger and garlic in a blender.

2. Heat the oil in a *kadhai*, add onion paste and green chillies. Cook until onion turns brown.

3. Add red chilli powder, coriander powder, *garam masala* and salt. Mix. Cook on medium heat until oil separates. Sprinkle a little water if the masala sticks to the pan.

4. Add *imli* pulp, coconut milk and 1 cup of water. Let it come to a boil. Add fish and cook on low heat for 10-12 minutes or until the fish is cooked. Remove from fire.

5. For the tempering, heat the oil in a frying pan add all the ingredients. When the seeds start spluttering pour over the hot fish. Serve hot.

Paneer Makhani

This classic makhani gravy is created out of pureed tomatoes, butter, milk, cream and ground cashews – a paneer dish fit for a five-star banquet.

Serves 4

250 gm cottage cheese (*paneer*) - cut into 1" long pieces

¼ cup cashewnuts (*kaju*) - soak in warm water for 15 minutes

5 large (500 gm) tomatoes - each cut into 4 pieces

2 tbsp clarified butter (*desi ghee*) or butter and 2 tbsp oil

4-5 flakes garlic and 1" piece ginger - ground to a paste (1½ tsp ginger-garlic paste)

1 tbsp dry fenugreek leaves (*kasoori methi*)

1 tsp tomato ketchup, ½ tsp cumin seeds (*jeera*)

2 tsp coriander (*dhania*) powder, ½ tsp *garam masala*

1 tsp salt, or to taste, ½ tsp red chilli powder, preferably paprika (*degi mirch*)

½ cup water, ½-1 cup milk, approx., ½ cup cream (optional)

1. Drain cashewnuts. Grind in a mixer to a very smooth paste using about 2 tbsp water.

2. Boil tomatoes in ½ cup water. Simmer for 4-5 minutes till soft. Remove from fire and cool. Grind the tomatoes along with the water to a smooth puree.

3. Heat oil and ghee or butter in a *kadhai*. Reduce heat. Add cumin. When it turns golden, add ginger-garlic paste. When paste starts to change colour add the above tomato puree and cook till dry. Add dry fenugreek leaves and tomato ketchup.

4. Add masalas — coriander powder, *garam masala*, salt and red chilli powder. Mix well for a few seconds. Cook till oil separates.

5. Add cashew paste. Mix well for 2 minutes. Add water. Boil. Simmer on low heat for 4-5 minutes. Reduce heat.

6. Add the *paneer* cubes. Remove from fire. Keep aside to cool for about 5 minutes.

7. Add enough milk to the cold *paneer* masala to get a thick curry, mix gently. (Remember to add milk only after the masala is no longer hot, to prevent the milk from curdling. After adding milk, heat curry on low heat.) Heat on low heat, stirring continuously till just about to boil.

8. Add cream, keeping the heat very low and stirring continuously. Remove from fire immediately and transfer to a serving dish. Serve hot.

Achaari Paneer

Pickling spices give a distinct personality – the rest of the flavours provide a harmonious balance – you will be proud of this presentation!

Serves 6

300 gm cottage cheese (*paneer*) - cut into 1½" cubes

2 capsicums - cut into 1" pieces, 2 tsp ginger-garlic paste

1 cup curd - beat well till smooth in a mixer, 4 tbsp oil

3 onions - chopped finely, 4 green chillies - chopped

½ tsp turmeric (*haldi*) powder, 1 tsp salt or to taste

1 tsp dried mango powder (*amchoor*) or lemon juice to taste

¾ tsp *garam masala*, 2-3 green chillies - cut lengthwise into 4 pieces

¼ cup milk, 2-3 tbsp cream, optional

ACHAARI MASALA

2 tsp *saunf*, 1 tsp *rai*, 1 tsp *jeera*

a pinch of *methi daana*, ½ tsp onion seeds (*kalonji*)

1. Cut *paneer* into 1½" cubes. Sprinkle ½ tsp haldi, a pinch of salt and ½ tsp red chilli powder on the *paneer* and capsicum pieces. Mix well. Keep aside for 10 minutes.

2. Collect all seeds of the achaari masala — *saunf, rai, methi daana, kalonji* and *jeera* together.

3. Heat 4 tbsp oil. Add the collected seeds together to the hot oil. Let them crackle for 1 minute or till cumin turns golden.

4. Add onions and chopped green chillies. Cook till onions turn golden.

5. Add turmeric and garlic-ginger paste. Mix well.

6. Reduce heat. Beat curd with 2 tbsp water and a pinch of haldi till smooth. Add gradually and keep stirring. Add *amchoor, garam masala* and salt or to taste. Cook for 2-3 minutes on low heat till the curd dries up a little. (Do not make it very dry). Remove from fire and let it cool down.

7. At the time of serving, add milk and slit green chillies. Add capsicum. Boil on low heat for a minute, stirring continuously. Cook on low flame for 2-3 minutes.

8. Add cream and *paneer* and cook for 1-2 minutes on low flame. Serve.

Chicken Korma

Serves 2-3

250 gm chicken with bones (leg pieces mostly used), 1 onion - finely sliced

MARINADE (MIX TOGETHER)

¼ cup cashews (*kaju*) and 2 tbsp white sesame seeds (*til*) – soaked in warm water for 15 minutes and ground to a paste

¼ cup yogurt (*dahi*) - whisk till smooth, 1 tbsp lemon juice

a pinch nutmeg (*jaiphal*) powder, 1 tsp ginger paste, 2 tsp garlic paste ½ tsp red chilli powder

¼ tsp turmeric (*haldi*) power, 1 tsp salt, ½ tsp garam masala

SABOOT GARAM MASALA (WHOLE SPICES)

2 green cardamoms (*chhoti illaichi*), 1 brown cardamom (*moti illaich i*), 2 cloves (*laung*)

1 bay leaf (*tej patta*), ¼ tsp crushed mace (*javitri*), 1 blade of star anise

FINAL MASALA FOR SPRINKLING (CRUSHED TOGETHER TO A POWDER)

1 blade mace (*javitri*), seeds of 1 green cardamom (*chhoti illaichi*), 1 clove (*laung*)

1. Whisk yogurt. Grind cashews and sesame seeds with some water to a paste. Add to the yogurt. Add all the other ingredients of the marinade also to the yogurt. Add chicken in it, mix well and marinate for at least 30 minutes.

2. Heat 3 tbsp oil. Add all the *saboot garam masala* (whole spices) to the hot oil. Wait for 1 minute for them to get fragrant.

3. Add sliced onion and cook until soft. Do not brown onions or it will discolour the gravy.

4. Add chicken along with the marinade. Boil and simmer for 5 minutes. Add about 1 cup water and cook covered for 10 minutes or till chicken turns tender.

5. Add ¼ tsp *garam masala*, ¼ tsp lemon juice and coriander. Remove from heat and sprinkle the crushed spices.

Maharashtrian Toor Dal

A touch of sweet and sour ((jaggery and lemon) gives this delicious dal the distinctive touch of the food of Maharashtra.

Serves 2-3

½ cup yellow lentils (*toor dal*), ¾ tsp salt, or to taste, ½ tsp turmeric (*haldi*) powder

1 tbsp jaggery (*gur*), 1 tbsp lemon juice, or to taste

TEMPERING/*TADKA*

2 tbsp clarified butter (*ghee*), a pinch of asafoetida (*hing*), ½ tsp mustard seeds (*rai*), some curry leaves

1. Clean, wash dal. Soak dal in 1½ cups of water for half an hour. Drain. Pressure cook dal with 2 cups water, salt and turmeric on high flame till the first whistle and then simmer for 5 minutes. Remove from heat. After the pressure drops, add gur and ½ cup water. Mix well. Simmer for 2-3 minutes. Remove from heat. The consistency should be thick.

2. For *tadka*/tempering heat ghee, add asafoetida and mustard seeds. Let it crackle & add curry leaves & immediately add it to the dal. Squeeze lemon juice on it. Check taste. Serve with rice.

Chicken Madras

Serves 3-4

250 gm chicken with bones, 3 tbsp brown onion paste - (made from 2 sliced onions deep fried till brown and ground with 2 tbsp yogurt)

4 tbsp oil, 1 dry red chilli (*sabot lal mirch*), ¾ tsp cumin seeds (*jeera*)

1 tsp ginger, 2 tsp garlic paste, ½ tsp *Kashmiri degi mirch*, ¼ cup coconut milk

1 tsp salt, ¼ tsp garam masala, green coriander (*hara dhania*) chopped for garnish

PASTE

a tiny piece of dried coconut (*khopra*) - chopped (2 tbsp)

1 tsp coriander seeds (*saboot dhania*), 2 dry red chillies (*saboot lal mirch*)

¼ tsp black mustard seeds (*sarson*), 1 tsp oil, 1 tbsp cashews (*kaju*) - soaked in water

TEMPERING (*TADKA*)

1 tbsp oil, ¼ cup black mustard seeds (*sarson*), 6 to 7 curry leaves (*kari patta*)

1. For the paste, roast all ingredients of the paste, except cashews. Roast till fragrant. Cool and grind with the soaked cashews with ¼ cup water. Keep paste aside.

2. Heat oil in *kadhai*, add dry red chilli and cumin seeds when splitters, add brown onion paste + ginger-garlic paste. Cook for 1 minute.

3. Add chicken and bhuno for about 15 minutes, till chicken is 80% tender.

4. Add the prepared paste add *degi mirch*. Cook for 15 minutes on slow fire. Add coconut milk and salt. Bhuno for 5 minutes till coconut milk is absorbed. Add ½ cup water and cook till gravy thickens and leaves oil. Add green coriander and *garam masala*.

5. To serve, heat oil in a small pan. Add mustard seeds. After a few seconds, add curry leaves. When they turn translucent, remove from fire and pour the oil over the hot chicken in the serving dish.

Tawa Jhinga Masala

*Carom seeds and ginger elevate this prawn delicacy from the ordinary
to a gourmet masterpiece. So easy to make too!*

Serves 4

½ kg prawns - medium size

3 tbsp clarified butter (*ghee*)

1 tsp carom seeds (*ajwain*)

1 large onion - chopped (¾ cup)

2 green chillies - slit, deseed and chopped

½ tbsp chopped ginger, ½ tsp red chilli powder

¼ cup chopped coriander (*hara dhania*)

¾ cup ready-made tomato puree

salt to taste, ¼ cup cream

1 tbsp lemon juice, ½ tsp *garam masala*

1. Shell and devein the prawns. Wash and pat dry.

2. Heat ghee on a large *tawa* or a big pan, add prawns and saute over medium heat for 2-3 minutes till prawns change colour. Remove from *tawa*.

3. To the ghee in the same *tawa*, add carom seeds and when it begins to crackle, add onions, green chillies and ginger, saute for 3 minutes.

4. Add tomato puree and cook until oil separates.

5. Add red chilli and coriander, *cook* for ½ minute.

6. Add prawns. Stir.

7. Add cream, stirring continuously. Remove from fire Sprinkle lemon juice, *garam masala*, stir. Adjust the seasonings.

8. Remove to a dish and serve with any Indian bread of your choice.

Methi Chicken

1 chicken (800 gm) - cut into small pieces or use 800 gm boneless chicken pieces

4 cups finely chopped fresh fenugreek greens (*methi*)

2 cups curd - beat well till smooth

8-10 tbsp ghee/oil

2 large tomatoes - pureed in the mixer, 2 tsp salt, 1 tsp *garam masala*

GRIND TOGETHER

2 large onions, 3-4 green chillies (use according to taste), 1½" piece ginger, 6-7 flakes garlic

TOPPING

3-4 tbsp ghee, ½ tsp red chilli powder

1. Grind together onions, green chillies, garlic and ginger to a fine paste.

2. Heat oil/ghee. Add onion paste and fry the paste to a rich brown colour.

3. Add tomatoes, salt and *garam masala*. Cook till tomatoes turn dry and oil separates.

4. Add chicken and fry well for 5-6 minutes on medium heat.

5. Add chopped fresh fenugreek greens and curd. Stir till it boils.

6. Cook till nearly dry. Reduce heat and cook covered for 3-4 minutes on low heat for a few minutes till chicken turns tender.

7. When the chicken turns tender, remove from fire. Keep aside till serving time.

8. At serving time, heat 4 tbsp ghee. Add red chilli powder. Remove from fire. Pour directly over the hot chicken in the serving dish. Serve immediately.

Gobhi Fry

Cauliflower florets tossed in a delicious masala – everyone's favourite, at all times.

Serves 4

1 medium whole cauliflower (500 gm) - cut into medium size florets with stalks

MASALA

4 tbsp oil

3 onions - chopped, seeds of 1 brown cardamom (*moti illaichi*)

3-4 pepper corns (*saboot kali mirch*), 2 cloves (*laung*)

3 tomatoes - roughly chopped, 1" ginger - chopped

2 tbsp curd (*dahi*) - beat well till smooth, ½ tsp red chilli powder

½ tsp garam masala, ½ tsp turmeric (*haldi*), ½ tsp dried mango powder (*amchoor*)

1 tsp salt, or to taste

1. Break the cauliflower into medium size florets, keeping the stalk intact. Wash and pat dry on a kitchen towel.

2. Heat oil in a *kadhai* for deep frying. Add all the cauliflower pieces and fry to a light brown colour. Remove from oil and keep aside.

3. Heat 4 tbsp oil in a clean *kadhai*. Add black cardamom, pepper corns and cloves. After a minute, add chopped onion. Cook till onions turn golden brown.

4. Add chopped tomatoes and ginger. Cook for 4-5 minutes till they turn soft and masala turns little dry.

5. Add well beaten curd. Cook till masala turns reddish again.

6. Reduce heat. Add red chilli powder, *garam masala*, turmeric, *amchoor* and salt. Cook for 1 minute. Add ½ cup water to get a thick masala. Boil. Cook for 1 minute on low flame. Keep aside.

7. At the time of serving, heat the masala. Add the fried cauliflower pieces to the masala and mix well on low heat for 2 minutes till the vegetable gets well blended with the masala. Serve hot.

Kadhai Murg

The coating sauce made from tomatoes is enriched with cream and enlivened with fenugreek and coriander – wrap the sauce around the chicken pieces and please the crowds!

Serves 4-6

1 medium sized (800 gm) chicken - cut into 12 pieces

1 tbsp coriander seeds (*saboot dhania*), 3 whole, dry red chillies, 6-7 tbsp oil

½ tsp fenugreek seeds (*methi daana*), 3 large onions - cut into slices

15-20 flakes garlic - crushed & chopped, 1" piece of ginger - crushed to a paste

4 large tomatoes - chopped, ½ cup ready-made tomato puree or ¾ cup home-made puree

1 tsp red chilli powder, 1 tsp ground coriander (*dhania*), 2 tsp salt, or to taste

¼ tsp dried mango powder (*amchoor*), ½ tsp garam masala

½ cup chopped green coriander (*hara dhania*), 1 capsicum - cut into slices

1" piece ginger - cut into match sticks, 1-2 green chillies - cut into long slices

½ cup cream, optional

1. Put coriander seeds and whole red chillies on a *tawa*. Keep on fire and roast lightly till it just starts to change colour. Crush the coriander seeds on a *chakla-belan* (rolling board and pin) to split the seeds. Keep red chillies whole. Keep aside.

2. Heat oil in a *kadhai*. Reduce heat. Add fenugreek seeds and the roasted whole red chillies and stir for a few seconds till fenugreek seeds turns golden.

3. Add onion and cook on medium heat till light brown. Add garlic and ginger. Stir for 1 minute.

4. Add the crushed coriander seeds, red chilli powder and coriander powder.

5. Add chicken and bhuno for 10 minutes on high flame, stirring well so that chicken attains a nice golden brown colour.

6. Add chopped tomatoes. Cook for 4-5 minutes. Add salt, *amchoor* and *garam masala*. Cover and cook for 15-20 minutes or till tender, stirring occasionally.

7. Add tomato puree and chopped green coriander. Cook for 5 minutes.

8. Add the capsicum, ginger match sticks and green chilli slices. Mix well.

9. Reduce heat. Add cream. Mix well for 2-3 minutes and remove from fire. Serve hot.

Cabbage Peanut Poriyal

A dry, spicy and crunchy South Indian side dish.

Serves 4

½ kg cabbage (1 medium) - chopped finely, ½ cup peanuts (*moongphali*) - roasted

1½ tsp salt, or to taste

TEMPERING

4 tbsp oil, 1 tsp mustard seeds (*rai*), ½ tsp cumin seeds (*jeera*)

2 tsp split black gram (*dhuli urad dal*), 2 tsp bengal gram dal (*channa dal*)

2 dry, red chillies - broken into bits

½ tsp asafoetida (*hing*), ¼ cup curry leaves

PASTE (GRIND TOGETHER)

2 green chillies, 4-5 tbsp grated coconut - remove the brown skin and then grate

1 onion - chopped, 1 tsp cumin seeds (*jeera*)

2 tbsp curd (*dahi*)

1. Heat oil. Reduce heat. Add all ingredients of tempering.

2. When dals turn golden, add the chopped cabbage. Mix well.

3. Add salt and 2 tbsp water. Mix well.

4. Add peanuts. Cover and cook on low heat for 7-8 minutes till cabbage turns tender.

5. Add the coconut paste. Stir fry for 3-4 minutes. Serve hot.

Note: You can make any poriyal in the same way - carrot, beetroot or capsicum.

Chicken Tikka Masala

Dry chicken tikka covered with thick masala.
It can be served as a snack or as a side dish with the main meal.

Serves 4

CHICKEN TIKKA MARINADE

500 gm boneless chicken - cut into tikka size pieces

1 cup curd - hang in a muslin cloth for 15-20 minutes

1 tbsp oil, 2 tsp ginger-garlic paste, 1 tsp *tandoori masala*, ¼ tsp *kala namak*, ¼ tsp *garam masala*

½ tsp red chilli powder, 1 tsp salt, 2-3 drops of red colour

MASALA

5 tbsp oil, ½ tsp mustard seeds (*sarson*), cumin seeds (*jeera*)

2 onions - sliced, 3-4 flakes of garlic - crushed, 4 green chillies - finely chopped

4 tomatoes - blanched, 1 cup coconut milk

4 tbsp mint (*pudina*) leaves - finely chopped, 4 tbsp coriander (*hara dhania*) - finely chopped

3 tbsp lemon juice, 1 tsp salt, 1 tsp garam masala

1. To prepare chicken tikka, wash and pat dry chicken. Marinate in the marinade ingredients for 3-4 hours.

2. Cover a grill rack with aluminium foil and grease it with some oil. Place chicken on it. Cook in a preheated oven at 180°C till done and golden, for about 15-20 minutes. Baste with oil in between. Keep aside.

3. Heat 5 tbsp oil, add mustard seeds and cumin. Wait for 30 seconds. Add sliced onions and saute over medium heat until golden brown. Add crushed garlic and chopped green chillies. Mix well.

4. Add tomatoes, cook till oil separates.

5. Add coconut milk and bring to a boil, stirring continuously. Lower heat and cook for 5-6 minutes, or until thick. Keep masala aside.

6. At the time of serving, add the cooked chicken tikka to the masala. Mix well. Add chopped mint, coriander, lemon juice, salt and *garam masala*. Serve hot.

Special Mixed Subzi

2 tbsp oil, ½ tsp cumin seeds (*jeera*), ½ tsp mustard seeds (*sarson*), ½ tsp onion seeds (*kalonji*)
¼ tsp fenugreek seeds (*methi daana*), 15-20 curry leaves, 2 onions - cut into rings, ¼ tsp turmeric (*haldi*)

MIX TOGETHER
¾ cup ready-made tomato puree, 2 tsp tomato ketchup
2 tsp ginger-garlic paste or 2 tsp ginger-garlic - finely chopped
½ tsp red chilli powder, ½ tsp dried mango powder (*amchoor*)
1 tsp coriander (*dhania*) powder, 1 tsp salt

VEGETABLES
1 carrot - cut diagonally into thin slices, 10-12 french beans - sliced diagonally into 1" pieces
8-10 small florets (pieces) of cauliflower, 1 green capsicum - deseed and cut into thin fingers
½ cup shelled peas (*matar*) - boiled
1 long, firm tomato - cut into 4 and then cut into thin long pieces

1. Boil 4 cups water with 1 tsp salt and ½ tsp sugar. Add sliced carrots and beans after the water boils. Boil for 2 minutes till crisp-tender. Strain. Refresh in cold water.

2. Mix together — tomato puree, tomato ketchup, ginger, garlic, red chilli powder, coriander powder, *amchoor* and salt in a bowl. Keep aside.

3. Collect together — cumin, mustard seeds, onion seeds and fenugreek seeds. Keep aside. Heat 2 tbsp oil in a *kadhai*. Add the collected ingredients. When cumin turns golden, reduce heat and add curry leaves and stir for a few seconds.

4. Add onions and cook till golden. Add turmeric. Mix.

5. Add the tomato puree mixed with dry masalas and stir on medium heat for 2 minutes.

6. Add carrot, cauliflower and beans. Stir for 3-4 minutes.

7. Add the capsicum, peas and tomato. Stir till well blended. Remove from fire.

8. Transfer to a serving dish. Serve hot.

Murg Nizam

A semi-dry chicken 'masala' cooked with nuts (cashewnuts, peanuts and coconut) and sesame seeds.

Serves 6-7

800 gm chicken with bones - cut into 12 pieces

8 tbsp oil or ghee, ¼ cup cashewnuts (*Kaju*)

2 onions - chopped, 1 dry red chilli (*sookhi lal mirch*)

3" piece of ginger and 28-30 flakes of garlic -
grind to a paste in a mixer with 2 tbsp water

8 green chillies - slit, deseeded & chopped

2½ tsp salt or to taste, 1 tsp turmeric (*haldi*)

¼ cup peanuts (*moongphali*) - crushed coarsely

2 tbsp sesame seeds (*til*) - crushed coarsely

½ cup coconut - brown skin removed and grated

¾ cup yogurt (*dahi*) - beat well till smooth

1 tsp garam masala, 1 tbsp lemon juice
¼ cup chopped green coriander (*hara dhania*), ¼ cup chopped mint (*pudina*)

1. Heat oil & fry cashewnuts until golden brown. Remove cashewnuts from *kadhai* & keep aside.

2. Heat the left over oil again and add chopped onions and saute over medium heat until golden brown. Add dry red chilli.

3. Add the ginger-garlic paste, stir for a minute.,

4. Add green chillies, salt and turmeric. Mix.

5. Add the crushed peanuts, crushed til seeds and grated coconut, stir for a minute.

6. Now add chicken, bhuno for 6-8 minutes.

7. Reduce heat, add yogurt and bhuno for 3-4 minutes on medium heat, stirring.

8. Add about 1½ cups water, bring to a boil, simmer for 15-20 minutes, or until tender. Adjust the seasoning.

9. Sprinkle *garam masala*, *lemon juice*, coriander and mint. Remove to a dish and sprinkle fried cashewnuts.

Dum ki Arbi

*Arbi gets a gourmet image in this amazing curry, made with yogurt and boiled onion paste,
thickened with poppy seeds and cooked slowly and lovingly.*

Serves 4

400 gm colocasia (*arbi*)

2 tbsp poppy seeds (*khus khus*), 3 onions

1" piece of ginger, 12 flakes of garlic, 1 tsp cumin (*jeera*)

1 tsp coriander (*dhania*) powder

½ tsp red chilli powder, ½ tsp garam masala powder

1 tsp salt or to taste, ½ tsp turmeric (*haldi*) powder

4-6 green cardamoms (*chhoti illaichi*)

2 cups yogurt (*dahi*), a pinch of nutmeg (*jaiphal*) - grated

oil to deep fry

coriander leaves to garnish

1. Soak poppy seeds in ¼ cup water. Keep aside.

2. Peel and cut colocasia into 1" pieces. Deep fry in hot oil till golden brown.

3. Peel onions and cut into 4 pieces and put in a saucepan with 2 cups of water. Boil onions for 3-4 minutes till soft. Drain. Cool.

4. Grind the onion, soaked poppy seeds, ginger, garlic, coriander powder, red chilli powder, cumin, *garam masala*, salt and turmeric in a blender to a paste.

5. Heat 2 tbsp oil in a pan. Add green cardamom, stir for a minute.

6. Add prepared paste. Saute till light golden brown.

7. Mix yogurt with ½ cup water. Add the yogurt stirring continuously; bring it to a boil.

8. Add colocasia and grated nutmeg.

9. Cover the pan with a tight fitting lid and simmer for 15 minutes. Alternatively cover the pan with aluminium foil or seal the lid with wheat flour dough, so that the aroma is trapped in the pan and does not escape.

10. Garnish with coriander and serve.

Sindhi Curry

A medley of vegetables in a well seasoned tangy tomato gravy thickened with gram flour.

Serves 4

500 gm tomatoes

3 tbsp oil

1½ tsp mustard seeds (*rai*), 1 tsp cumin seeds (*jeera*)

½ cup gram flour (*besan*)

1 potato - chopped, 8 green chillies, 1 long, thin brinjal - chopped

3-4 guwar or French beans - chopped, 2 drumsticks - cut into 3" pieces

10-12 lady fingers - each cut into 2 pieces & fried in oil

½ tsp turmeric (*haldi*) powder, 2 tsp red chilli powder

6 kokums or a lemon-size ball of tamarind (*imli*) - soaked in ½ cup water

2 tbsp finely chopped coriander (*hara dhania*)

1½ tsp salt, or to taste

1. Boil tomatoes in 4 cups water for 3-4 minutes. Peel and puree in a mixer. Keep aside.

2. Heat 3 tbsp oil in a saucepan. Add rai and cumin. Add gram flour and roast over medium flame for 4-5 minutes till golden brown. Remove from heat. Add tomatoes and 4 cups of water.

3. Mix well. Heat again. When it begins to boil add all vegetables except lady's fingers.

4. Add haldi, red chillies and 2 cups water. Simmer for 10 minutes. Add kokums or tamarind pulp and boil for 5 minutes. Add salt, fried lady's fingers and coriander leaves. Serve.

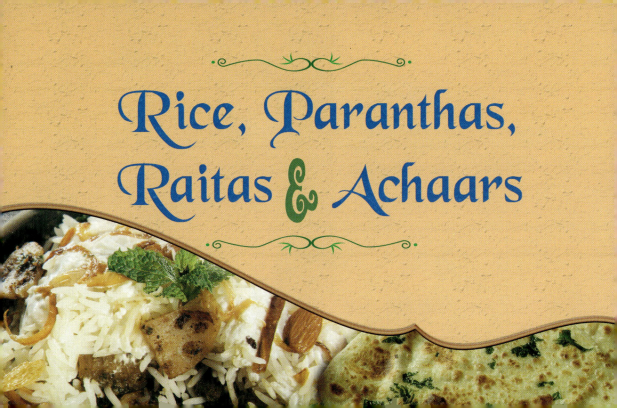

Rice, Paranthas, Raitas & Achaars

Hyderabadi Biryani

*Rice and chicken are cooked separately, and then they are layered together along with fried onions.
The pot is tightly sealed and steamed on low heat to allow all the flavours to blend.*

Serves 6-8

2 cups basmati rice, 1 tbsp oil, 2 bay leaves (*tej patta*), 1½ tsp salt

FOR THE CHICKEN
1 chicken (700-800 gm) - cut into 12 pieces, 4 large onions - chopped, 1½ tbsp ginger-garlic paste

2 large tomatoes - chopped, 1 cup yogurt, 5-6 tbsp oil, 1 tsp red chilli powder, salt to taste

GARNISHING
1 cup sliced onions - fried till crisp and brown (2-3 large onions), ½ cup mint leaves (*pudina*)

few strands saffron (*kesar*) soaked in 1 tsp water and 2 drops kewra essence

FLAVOURING MASALA
1½ tsp cumin (*jeera*), 3-4 green cardamoms (*chhoti illaichi*), 3-4 cloves (*laung*), 2" cinnamon (*dalchini*)

2-3 pepper corns (*saboot kali mirch*), 2 black cardamoms (*moti illaichi*), ¼ cup water

1. For rice, boil 7 cups of water with bay leaves, salt, and oil. Add rice and cook till almost tender. Strain and spread the drained rice on a wide tray. Run a fork on the rice to let steam escape.

2. For chicken, heat oil. Add onions. Stir fry till brown. Add ginger-garlic paste. Add tomatoes. Cook till dry. Add curd. Stir for 1 minute. Add salt, chilli powder and chicken. Bhuno for 8 minutes. Add 1 cup water Cook till tender. Remove from fire.

3. Grind all the ingredients for the flavouring masala in a blender to a paste. Strain it through a sieve. Keep liquid masala aside.

4. For assembling the biryani, take a large heavy-bottomed pan, sprinkle some curry of the chicken at the bottom. Spread some of the rice. Place ½ the chicken pieces on it and wet the rice with some curry. Sprinkle some fried onion and mint on it. Sprinkle 2-3 tbsp liquid flavouring masala. Repeat by adding rice, then chicken, followed by mint and fried onions and flavouring masala. Finish with a top layer of rice sprinkled with fried onions, mint, flavouring masala and *kesar* mixture. Mix slightly.

5. Cover the pan with a tight fitting lid and seal the lid with dough. Place the pan on fire with a *tawa* underneath to reduce the heat to minimum for ½ hour before serving.

Nan

Nans are oblong flat breads traditionally baked in a clay oven, tandoor, *but I have made them in an electric oven with equal success.*

Serves 4

2 cups (200 gm) plain flour (*maida*)

½ tsp baking soda (*mitha soda*)

½ tsp salt

½ tsp baking powder

½ cup hot milk

½ cup warm water, or as required

1 tsp onion seeds (*kalaunji*) or 1 tsp black or white sesame seeds (*til*)

1. Sift the flour, baking soda and salt together in a bowl.

2. Mix the baking powder into the hot milk and keep aside, undisturbed, for 1 minute. Bubbles will start appearing on the surface.

3. Add the milk to the flour and mix well. Knead, adding water, to make a soft dough. Continue to knead till the dough becomes smooth and elastic. Keep covered in a warm place for 3-4 hours to rise.

4. When it is time to serve the nans, divide the dough into 6-8 balls. Roll out each ball to an oblong shape. Sprinkle some nigella or sesame seeds and press them down with the rolling pin. Pull one side of the nan to give it the traditional pointed shape.

5. Apply some water on the back of the nan and press it on the walls of a hot tandoor. Alternately, cover the rack of the oven with aluminium foil and place the nans on it. Bake them in a very hot oven. When light brown spots appear on the surface, turn the nans and cook till done. Smear some butter on the hot nans and serve with dals or curries.

Kashmiri Gosht Pulao

Unlike a biryani, a pulao does not need layering since the rice cooks in the mutton stock and absorbs all the flavours fully.

Serves 5-6

500 gm mutton, preferably mutton, with very little bones - wash well

2½ cups basmati rice - washed and soaked for 30 minutes, 5-6 tbsp ghee

2 onions - sliced, 3 green chillies - chopped, 1 tsp ginger paste, 1 cup yogurt (*dahi*), 3 tsp salt

KHUS KHUS PASTE

1½ tbsp poppy seeds (*khus-khus*) - soaked in warm water for ½ hour, 1½ tbsp fennel (*saunf*) powder

seeds of 8 green cardamoms (*chhoti illaichi*) and 2 black cardamoms (*moti illaichi*), 8 cloves (*laung*)

½ tsp cumin seeds (*jeera*), 8-10 pepper corns (*saboot kali mirch*), 2" stick of cinnamon (*dalchini*)

1. Wash rice and preferably soak for 30 minutes.

2. Put mutton, 1 tsp salt & 5 cups water in a pressure cooker. Pressure cook to give 4-5 whistles. Reduce heat and keep on low heat for 5 minutes. Mutton should be tender. (The number of whistles will depend on the quality of mutton). Remove from fire.

3. Grind all ingredients for the khus khus paste together to a fine paste in a mixer. Keep aside.

4. Heat ghee in a heavy-bottomed pan. Add sliced onion. Fry till brown.

5. Add ginger paste and green chillies. Mix well.

6. Add mutton pieces (without the stock). Add yogurt. Mix well. Fry for 5-6 minutes. Add the freshly made khus khus paste to the mutton. Mix well.

7. Measure the mutton stock and add water if required to make it to 4½ cups.

8. Add rice and 2 tsp salt. Add 4½ cups stock. Boil.

9. Cover and cook on low heat till rice is well cooked and the water dries up. Separate with a fork. Serve hot.

Jalpari Biryani

Serves 4

125 gm *bhein* or lotus stem (*kamal kakri*)

1 cup basmati rice - soaked for 20-30 minutes, ½ tsp salt, 4 cups water

3-4 green cardamoms (*chhoti illaichi*), 1 black cardamom (*moti illaichi*), ½" stick cinnamon (*dalchini*)

MINT PASTE (GRIND TOGETHER)

2-3 tbsp mint leaves (*pudina*), 4 tbsp coriander chopped, 1 green chilli

MASALA

3 onions, 1" piece ginger, ½ tsp red chilli powder, 1 tbsp raisin (*kishmish*)

½ cup curd (*dahi*) - well beaten & mixed with ¼ cup water

OTHER INGREDIENTS

2 tbsp chopped mint leaves (*pudina*), 2 onions - sliced and deep fried till brown

½ cup curd (*dahi*) - well beaten, 2 pinches of mace (*javitri*) - crushed and powdered

seeds of 2 green cardamoms (*chhoti illaichi*) - powdered

1. Peel lotus stem. Cut into thin diagonal slices and soak slices in water. Keep aside.

2. Prepare mint paste by grinding all the ingredients of the paste together.

3. Grind onions, ginger and red chilli powder together to a paste.

4. Heat 1 *karchhi* (4-5 tbsp oil) in a *handi* or a heavy bottomed pan. Add the onion paste. Cook on low flame till light brown and oil separates.

5. Add raisin and stir for ½ a minute.

6. Reduce flame. Add beaten curd mixed with a little water, stirring continuously to prevent curd from curdling. Stir till masala turns thick.

7. Drain lotus stem and add to the masala. Add 1 tsp salt. Bhuno for 4-5 minutes.

8. Add 1 cup water. Cover with a tight fitting lid and cook on low flame for 15 minutes or till soft. The lotus stem should not taste raw, although it may taste a little hard.

9. Add mint paste. Bhuno for 5-7 minutes, remove from fire and keep aside. Keep lotus stem aside.

10. To prepare the rice, boil 4 cups water with all the *saboot garam masala* and salt.

11. Drain the soaked rice and add to boiling water. Keep checking and feeling a grain of rice in between the finger and thumb to see if it is done. Boil on medium flame for 7-8 minutes till the rice is nearly done. Take care to see that the rice is not over cooked.

12. Strain rice in a rice strainer or colander. Keep aside uncovered for 10 minutes. Then spread the rice in a big tray.

13. Deep fry 2 sliced onions to a crisp brown colour. Keep aside.

14. Beat ½ cup curd. Add crushed and powdered mace and green cardamom to the curd. Keep aside.

15. Finely chop 2 tbsp mint leaves and keep aside.

16. To assemble the biryani, put half the vegetable with the masala in a *handi*.

17. Spread half the rice over it. Spoon half the flavoured curd over it.

18. Sprinkle some fried onions and chopped mint leaves. Repeat the masala vegetable and the other layers.

19. Cover the *handi*. Seal with *atta* dough and keep on dum for 15-20 minutes in a slow oven (100°C). Break the seal just before serving.

Lachha Pudina Parantha

The flavour of mint is crusted right on top of this so-easy-to-make flaky parantha, making every bite a pure delight!

Makes 6

4 tbsp freshly chopped or dry mint leaves (*pudina*), 2 cups whole wheat flour (*atta*)
1 tsp carom seeds (*ajwain*), 2 tbsp oil, ½ tsp salt, ½ tsp red chilli powder

1. Mix *atta* with all ingredients except mint. Add enough water to make a dough of rolling consistency. Make walnut-sized balls. Roll out to make a thick chappati.

2. Spread 1 tsp of ghee all over. Cut a slit from the outer edge till the centre.

3. Start rolling from the slit to form a cone. Keeping the cone upright, press cone gently.

4. Roll out to a thick *roti*. Sprinkle pudina. Press with the *belan* (rolling pin).

5. Cook on a *tawa*, frying on both sides or apply some water on the back side of the parantha and stick it in a hot tandoor. Serve hot.

Anda Parantha

Slip an egg into the pocket of a potato-stuffed parantha & let it set – a fantastic treat for hungry tummies!

Serves 6

DOUGH

2 cups whole wheat flour (*atta*)

2 tbsp oil

¾ tsp salt, ½ tsp red chilli powder

½ tsp carom seeds (*ajwain*)

½ tsp cumin (*jeera*) powder

OTHER INGREDIENTS

4 eggs

2 potatoes - boiled and mashed

salt to taste, ½ tsp red chilli powder

½ tsp garam masala, oil or ghee for frying

1. Mix *atta*, oil, salt, red chilli powder, carom seeds and cumin powder. Knead with enough water to a dough of rolling consistency. Cover and keep aside for 15 minutes.

2. Mix potatoes with salt, red chilli powder and garam masala.

3. Make 4 balls from the dough. Roll out a ball to a diameter of 5" like the size of a poori.

4. Put a heaped tbsp of mashed potatoes (about ¼ of the mixture) in the centre. Collect the sides of the rolled out dough to cover the filling.

5. Flatten the stuffed ball slightly and press over dry flour. Roll out to a slightly thick parantha.

6. Carefully pick up the parantha and put it on a hot griddle (*tawa*). When the underside is cooked, turn to cook the other side. Smear some oil or ghee on the parantha. Trickle some oil on the sides too, around the edges. Turn the parantha to make it light golden.

7. When the parantha is almost done, shut off the fire. Make a 3-4" slit, a little away from the edge of the parantha. Open up the parantha from the slit with the help of a knife to get a pocket. Break a whole egg in a small bowl. Put the egg all together in the pocket of the parantha. Return to low heat and let the egg in the parantha cook for 2-3 minutes on low heat. Remove parantha from *tawa* when crisp and golden brown on both sides. Serve hot.

Tandoori Keema Parantha

Tasty and juicy chicken keema makes mouth-watering layers in this incredibly flaky parantha cooked in a tandoor or oven.

Makes 6

FILLING

250 gm chicken mince (*keema*), 2 tbsp oil

1 onion - chopped finely, 2 tsp finely chopped ginger

1 tsp salt, 1 tsp coriander (*dhania*) powder

½ tsp red chilli powder, ½ tsp garam masala

2 green chillies - chopped

1 tbsp finely chopped fresh coriander

1 tbsp dried fenugreek leaves (*kasoori methi*)

DOUGH

2 cups whole wheat flour (*atta*), ½ tsp salt, 1 tbsp *ghee*

1. To prepare the dough, sift flour and salt. Rub in 1 tbsp ghee. Add enough water to make a dough. Keep aside for 30 minutes.

2. To prepare the filling, heat 2 tbsp of oil and stir fry the chopped onions until brown.

3. Add mince and ginger and cook for 3-4 minutes. Add salt, coriander powder, red chilli powder and *garam masala*. Fry for 1-2 minutes. Cook covered on low heat for about 5 minutes, till the mince is cooked. Add green chillies and 1 tbsp finely chopped coriander. If there is any water, uncover and dry the mince on fire. Keep the filling aside.

4. Divide the dough into 6 equal parts. Shape into round balls. Flatten each ball, roll out each into a round of 5" diameter. Spread 1 tsp ghee. Then spread 1-2 tbsp of filling all over.

5. Make a slit, starting from the centre till any one end. Start rolling from the slit, to form an even cone. Keeping the cone upright, press slightly.

6. Roll out, sprinkle some dried fenugreek leaves and press. Apply water on the back side of the parantha and stick carefully in a heated tandoor or place in a preheated oven in a greased tray.

7. Remove after a few minutes. Spread some ghee, serve hot.

Southern Tomato Rice

Cooked rice is tossed in a spicy tomato base till it soaks up all the flavours.

Serves 3-4

1 cup basmati rice

4 small tomatoes - ground to a puree in a mixi

2-3 onions - chopped

¼ tsp turmeric (*haldi*) powder

1½ tsp salt or to taste, 1 tsp red chilli powder

¼ tsp asafoetida (*hing*) powder

TEMPERING

3 tbsp oil

1 tsp mustard seeds (*sarson*)

1 tbsp gram lentils (*channe ki dal*)

few curry leaves

1. Clean and wash rice. Boil 5-6 cups water in a large pan. Add rice. Cook till done.

2. Strain the rice in a colander (big metal strainer). Keep aside to cool by spreading the rice in a big tray.

3. Heat oil in a *kadhai*. Reduce flame. Add hing powder. Add sarson and dal. Cook on very low flame till dal changes colour.

4. Add curry leaves and onions. Fry till onions turn light brown.

5. Add tomato puree.

6. Add turmeric, salt and red chilli powder.

7. Cook on low flame till the dal turns soft and the tomatoes turn absolutely dry and oil separates.

8. Separate the rice grains with a fork and add to the tomatoes. Stir carefully till well mixed. Serve hot.

Baingan ka Raita

Cool and pure yogurt is contrasted with tingling mustard seeds, curry leaves and red chillies – with slices of fried brinjals stirred in, this makes the perfect raita.

Serves 4

1 small thin, long aubergine (*baingan*)

1 tsp chaat masala

2 cups yogurt (*dahi*)

1 tsp salt, oil to shallow fry

FOR TEMPERING (*TADKA*)

1 tbsp oil

1 tbsp black mustard (*sarson*) seeds

6-8 curry leaves (*curry patta*)

2 whole dry red chillies (*saboot sookhi lal mirch*)

1. Wash and cut the aubergine into thin round slices.

2. Heat the oil in a non-stick frying pan; add aubergine, fry till light brown. Sprinkle *chaat masala*. Remove.

3. Beat yogurt with salt. Pour into a serving bowl. Add baingan. Mix gently.

4. For the tempering, heat the oil and all ingredients of the tadka, wait for a minute. Immediately pour over the yogurt. Serve chilled.

Beetroot Raita

We have used beetroot in our raita, believe me it's delicious.
The colour darkens on keeping, so use less beetroot.

Serves 3

1 cup (250 gm) yogurt (*dahi*)

½ of a small beetroot - boiled, peeled & grated

½ tsp roasted cumin (*bhuna jeera*) powder

a pinch of red chilli powder

a pinch of salt, ½ tsp sugar

1. Beat yogurt till smooth. Add cumin, chilli powder, salt and sugar. Mix.

2. Add just enough beet, about 1-2 tbsp only to get a nice pink colour. Check taste. Serve chilled.

Chicken Achaar

All the traditional pickling spices are used – but when the main ingredient is chicken, you have something fantastically different!

Serves 8

½ kg boneless chicken - cut into 1" pieces

1 tsp red chilli powder, ½ tsp turmeric (*haldi*), 1 tsp salt

1½ tbsp garlic paste, 1½ tbsp ginger paste

1½ cups mustard oil, ½ tsp asafoetida (*hing*), 1 big onion - chopped (¾ cup)

1 cup (200 ml) malt vinegar

SPICES FOR ACHAAR

seeds of 1 black cardamom (*moti illaichi*) & seeds of 2 green cardamoms (*chhoti illaichi*) - powdered,

¾ tsp salt, 2 tsp fennel seeds (*saunf*) - powdered

½ tbsp black cumin seeds (*shah jeera*), ½ tsp fenugreek seeds (*methi daana*)

1¼ tsp mustard seeds (*rai*), 2 bay leaves (*tej patta*)

1. Mix chicken with red chilli powder, turmeric, salt, half of ginger and garlic pastes. Keep aside for 30 minutes.

2. Heat oil in a *kadhai*/wok to a smoking point, reduce to medium heat and deep fry the marinated chicken pieces for 2-3 minutes. Remove chicken and strain the oil.

3. Collect all the achaar spices together and keep aside.

4. Heat the strained oil in a separate *kadhai*/wok, add hing, stir for 15 seconds, add onions and deep fry until golden brown. Then add the remaining ginger and garlic pastes, stir for 2 minutes. Add the collected achaar spices and stir for ½ minute.

5. Add vinegar. Bring to a boil, add the fried chicken and stir over high heat for 3-4 minutes. Remove and cool.

6. Transfer to a sterilized earthenware or glass jar, secure with muslin cloth around the opening of the jar and leave it in the sun or in a warm place for 2 days. Remove the muslin and cover with a lid. Consume within 60 days.

Note: Ensure all moisture is removed from the chicken before pickling. The presence of moisture induces fungal growth and reduces shelf life.

Prawn Balchao

Serve this at room temperature as a very special achaar – or serve hot as an exclusive and elegant side dish – either way you have a winner!

Serves 12

1 kg prawns (small size)

oil to deep fry prawns, 150 ml/2/3 cup oil

1 cup chopped onions, ½ cup chopped tomatoes

10 curry leaves (*curry patta*), 2½ tsp sugar, salt to taste

PASTE

20 whole red chillies

4" stick of cinnamon (*dalchini*)

15 green cardamoms (*chhoti illaichi*)

15 cloves (*laung*), 1 tsp pepper corns (*saboot kali mirch*), 1 tsp cumin seeds (*jeera*)

1 tbsp chopped garlic, 3 tbsp chopped ginger, ¾ cup malt vinegar, 1 tsp mustard seeds (*rai*)

1. Shell and devein the prawns. Wash and pat dry.

2. Heat oil in a *kadhai* and deep fry prawns for 2 minutes. Remove from oil.

3. Grind all ingredients of paste to a smooth paste in a blender.

4. Heat oil in a *kadhai* or wok, add onions and saute over medium heat until golden brown.

5. Add tomatoes, stir for 2- 3 minutes.

6. Add the paste and cook for 5-6 minutes.

7. Add prawns and stir for 2 minutes.

8. Add curry leaves and sugar, stir. Add salt to taste. Serve at room temperature.

Desserts

Shahi Tukri Lajawaab

In this innovative interpretation of a traditional dessert, fried bread is soaked in a mixture of sweetened, thickened milk cooked with grated paneer.

Serves 8-10

6 slices of bread - sides removed & each cut into 4 pieces & deep fried till golden brown

5 tbsp of chopped mixed nuts (*badaam, kishmish, pista* etc.), ¾ cup cold milk

PANEER LAYER

4 cups milk, ¾ cup sugar

¾ tsp green cardamom (*chhoti illaichi*) powdered

8 tsp cornflour dissolved in ½ cup milk

100 gm cottage cheese (*paneer*) - grated

2 drops of *kewra* essence

1. For the *paneer* layer, boil 4 cups milk. Simmer on low flame for 20 minutes.

2. In the meanwhile, boil sugar with ½ cup water in a separate pan. Keep on low heat for 5 minutes. Add grated *paneer*. Cook for 1 minute. Remove from fire.

3. Add cornflour paste to milk of step 1, stirring continuously. Keep stirring for 2 minutes till thick.

4. Add the prepared sugar and *paneer* mixture. Boil. Keep on heat for 1 minute. Remove from fire. Cool. Add essence. Sprinkle cardamom powder. Keep aside.

5. Remove the side crusts of bread. Cut each slice into 4 square pieces. Heat oil in a *kadhai*. Deep fry each piece till golden brown. Let it cool. Dip each piece of bread for a second in some cold milk, put in a small flat dish. Remove immediately. Take a serving dish. Spread 1 tbsp of *paneer* layer at the bottom of the dish. Place pieces of fried bread together in a single layer to cover the base of the dish.

6. Spread about 1 tsp of the *paneer* mixture on each piece. Sprinkle 1 tsp of chopped mixed nuts on the *paneer*. Repeat the bread layer in the same way with bread pieces first then the *paneer* layer and finally top with chopped mixed nuts.

7. Repeat with the left over bread, *paneer* and nuts to get a 3 layered pudding. Cover with a cling wrap (plastic film) and let it set for at least ½ hour before serving. Serve at room temperature.

Payasam

Fine vermicelli is cooked in ghee, sugar and milk then garnished with fried nuts & raisins.

Serves 6

4 cups milk

½ cup water

¾ cup sugar, or to taste

1 cup broken vermicelli (*seviyaan*)

2 tbsp *ghee*

a large pinch of saffron (*kesar*), optional

1 tbsp broken cashewnut pieces (*kaju tukda*)

2 tbsp raisins (*kishmish*)

3-4 seeds of green cardamoms (*chhoti illaichi*) - powdered

a few drops rose essence

1. Heat ghee. Fry cashewnut pieces and raisins, remove, set aside.
2. Add seviyaan to the pan, fry to a light brown, add water, cook for just a minute, on low heat.
3. Now add the milk gradually, stirring.
4. Add sugar, continue to cook until payasam is quite thick. Remove from fire. Check sugar.
5. Add cardamom, nuts and raisins. Add rose essence, mix thoroughly. Serve hot or cold.

Note: You could add a large pinch of kesar along with milk while it is boiling, then omit rose essence.

Saffron Kulfi Falooda

The delicious Indian Ice cream topped with sweetened thin vermicelli. Saffron lends it's flavour and colour to this most popular Indian dessert. Pistachios and almonds add to the richness.

Serves 6-8

1 kg (4 cups) low fat milk, 5 tbsp skimmed milk powder

3 tbsp cornflour, ¼ cup sugar, 6-7 strands saffron (*kesar*)

3-4 green cardamoms (*chhoti illaichi*) - crushed

1 tbsp shredded pistachios (*pista*), 1 tbsp shredded almonds (*badaam*)

FALOODA

1 cup thin rice vermicelli, 3-4 strands saffron (*kesar*), 3 tbsp sugar, 2 green cardamoms (*chhoti illaichi*)

1. Dissolve cornflour and milk powder in ½ cup milk to a paste. Heat the rest of the milk with sugar and *kesar*. Add the paste gradually, stirring continuously. Mix well. Add crushed seeds of green cardamom. Boil. Simmer on low heat, for about 15 minutes till slightly thick.

2. Cool. Add pistachios and almonds. Fill in clean kulfi moulds and leave to set in the freezer for 6-8 hours or overnight.

3. To prepare the falooda boil 4 cups water. Add the rice vermicelli. Boil. Simmer on low heat for 2-3 minutes till the vermicelli turns soft and no crunch remains. Strain. Add cold water to refresh. Strain again.

4. Make a sugar syrup by boiling ¾ cup water, 3 tbsp sugar, *kesar* and green cardamom together. Simmer for a couple of minutes. Remove from heat and put in the boiled vermicelli. Keep soaked in sugar syrup, in the refrigerator, till serving time.

5. To serve, remove the kulfi from the mould, cut into two halves lengthways and top with some falooda (without the syrup). Serve.

Khajur Tukri

250 gm dates (*khajur*) - deseeded & chopped

¾ cup bengal gram dal (*channe ki dal*)

2½ cups milk

½ cup melted desi ghee or oil (do not take used oil, take fresh oil)

2-3 tbsp chopped mixed nuts (*badaam*, *kaju*, *pista*)

1 tbsp melon seeds (*magaz*) (optional)

1 tbsp sugar

seeds of 3-4 green cardamoms (*chhoti illaichi*) - crushed

1. Wash and soak dal with enough water to cover. Keep aside for 30 minutes.

2. Soak the chopped dates in ½ cup hot milk. Keep aside.

3. Drain the water from the dal. Put it in a heavy bottomed *kadhai*. Add 2 cups milk to the dal. Keep on fire. Bring to a boil. Cook for about 20 minutes or till dal turns soft and about ½ cup milk remains.

4. Remove dal from fire and let it cool down.

5. Churn the dates along with the milk in which they were soaked to a paste. Remove from mixer to a bowl.

6. Churn the dal also along with the milk to a paste. Keep aside.

7. Heat ½ cup ghee or oil in a clean *kadhai*. Add chopped nuts and magaz. Stir for 2 minutes till golden.

8. Add the dal paste to the ghee and bhuno for 10 minutes till golden. Add the date paste also. Bhuno on medium flame for about 10 minutes or till ghee separates.

9. Add sugar and cardamom powder, mix well till sugar dissolves.

10. Spread mixture on the backside of a *thali* to a rectangle of about ½" thickness. Give it a neat square shape with the help of a knife.

11. Let it set. Cut into diamond shape pieces and serve.

Malpuas

These pancakes are soaked in syrup, making them one of the best desserts for people with a sweet tooth. Prepare the batter at least one hour before frying the malpuas.

Gives 12-14 small malpuas

BATTER

1 cup flour (*maida*)

2 tbsp whole wheat flour (*atta*)

1 cup cream (*malai*)

½ cup milk (as much as required)

ghee for frying

SUGAR SYRUP

1 cup sugar, ½ cup water

a few strands saffron or 1-2 drops yellow food colour

1-2 green cardamoms (*chhoti illaichi*) - powdered

1. Mix all the ingredients well so that no lumps remain. The batter should be a little thicker than a cake batter. It should be of a soft dropping consistency. A thin batter will spread.

2. Leave aside for 1-2 hours. (very essential)

3. Heat ghee for deep frying in a nonstick frying pan.

4. With the help of a spoon drop a spoonful of batter in moderately hot ghee. Spread to get a small round malpua. Put as many (about 4-5) malpuas as the pan can hold.

5. Fry on both sides to golden brown. Drain and keep aside.

6. Mix sugar, water and all other ingredients for sugar syrup in a pan. Boil for 3-4 minutes to get one thread consistency syrup.

7. Drop malpuas in hot syrup, 2-3 at a time. Give 1-2 boils. Remove with a slotted spoon so that excess syrup is drained.

8. Place on a serving dish garnished with chopped almonds and pistas. Serve plain or with rabri or kheer.

Note: Malpuas can be fried in advance and kept without sugar syrup in an airtight box in the fridge for 1-2 days. At the time of serving drop into hot sugar syrup, give 1-2 boils and serve hot.

Badaam ka Halwa

If you are looking for pure pleasure try this halwa! Almond paste and khoya sautéed in ghee, then cooked with sugar and milk.

Serves 4

150 gm (1 cup) almonds (*badaam*)

200 gm *khoya* - grate or crumble

1 cup sugar

1 cup milk

15 gm (1 tbsp) clarified butter (*desi ghee*)

seeds of 2 green cardamoms (*chhoti illaichi*) - powdered

1. Soak almonds in water for 2-3 hours or overnight. Remove peel and grind to a paste. Keep almond paste aside.

2. Heat ghee in a heavy-bottom pan.

3. Add khoya, cook on low heat for about 4-5 minutes, till light golden.

4. Add almond paste cook for about 4-5 minutes, till khoya becomes golden.

5. Add sugar. Stir for 3-4 minutes on low flame.

6. Add milk and illaichi powder. Cook till halwa leaves ghee, approx. 10 minutes. Garnish with almonds.

Glossary of Names/Terms

Appetizers	Small tasty bits of food served before meals.
Aubergine	Brinjal/eggplant
Au gratin	Any dish made with white sauce and covered with cheese and then baked or grilled.
Baste	To brush the food with some fat during cooking in the oven, to keep it moist and soft.
Batter	Any mixture of flour and a liquid which is beaten or stirred to make a pouring consistency.
Bell peppers	Capsicums
Blanch	To remove skin by dipping into hot water for a couple of minutes. e.g. to blanch tomatoes or almonds.
Curry powder	A blend of Indian spices.
Desiccated coconut	Powdered coconut.
Dice	To cut into small neat cubes.
Dough	A mixture of flour, liquid etc., kneaded together into a stiff paste or roll.
Drain	To remove liquid from food.
Marinate	To soak food in a mixture for some time so that flavours penetrates into the food.
Minced	Very finely chopped.
Okra	A green vegetable, also called lady finger.
Plain flour	All purpose flour, *maida*.
Saute	To toss and make light brown in shallow fat.
Soup cubes	Flavourful cubes added to soups or sauces. Also called seasoning cubes or stock cubes.
Tofu	Cheese prepared by curdling soya bean milk.

INTERNATIONAL CONVERSION GUIDE

These are not exact equivalents; they've been rounded-off to make measuring easier.

WEIGHTS & MEASURES

METRIC	IMPERIAL
15 g	½ oz
30 g	1 oz
60 g	2 oz
90 g	3 oz
125 g	4 oz (¼ lb)
155 g	5 oz
185 g	6 oz
220 g	7 oz
250 g	8 oz (½ lb)
280 g	9 oz
315 g	10 oz
345 g	11 oz
375 g	12 oz (¾ lb)
410 g	13 oz
440 g	14 oz
470 g	15 oz
500 g	16 oz (1 lb)
750 g	24 oz (1½ lb)
1 kg	30 oz (2 lb)

LIQUID MEASURES

METRIC	IMPERIAL
30 ml	1 fluid oz
60 ml	2 fluid oz
100 ml	3 fluid oz
125 ml	4 fluid oz
150 ml	5 fluid oz (¼ pint/1 gill)
190 ml	6 fluid oz
250 ml	8 fluid oz
300 ml	10 fluid oz (½ pint)
500 ml	16 fluid oz
600 ml	20 fluid oz (1 pint)
1000 ml	1¾ pints

CUPS & SPOON MEASURES

METRIC	IMPERIAL
1 ml	¼ tsp
2 ml	½ tsp
5 ml	1 tsp
15 ml	1 tbsp
60 ml	¼ cup
125 ml	½ cup
250 ml	1 cup

HELPFUL MEASURES

METRIC	IMPERIAL
3 mm	1/8 in
6 mm	¼ in
1 cm	½ in
2 cm	¾ in
2.5 cm	1 in
5 cm	2 in
6 cm	2½ in
8 cm	3 in
10 cm	4 in
13 cm	5 in
15 cm	6 in
18 cm	7 in
20 cm	8 in
23 cm	9 in
25 cm	10 in
28 cm	11 in
30 cm	12 in (1ft)

BEST SELLERS BY
SNAB
Excellence in Books

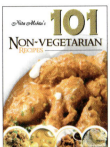

101 Non-Vegetarian Recipes

Indian Favourites (Veg. & Non-Veg)

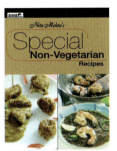

SPECIAL Non-Vegetarian Recipes

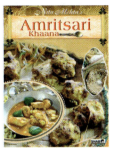

Amritsari Khaana

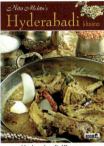

Hyderabadi Khaana

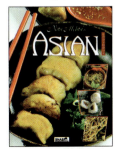

Asian Cookbook

Fish & Prawns

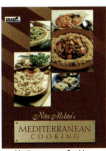

Mediterranean Cooking

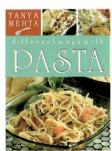

Different ways with Pasta

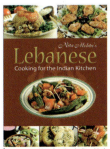

Lebanese cooking for the Indian kitchen

BEST SELLERS BY SNAB
Excellence in Books

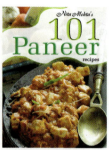

101 Paneer Recipes

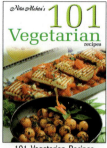

101 Vegetarian Recipes

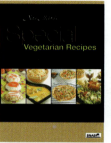

SPECIAL Vegetarian Recipes

Cakes & Cake Decorations

101 Diet Recipes

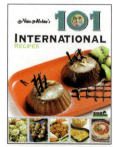

101 International Recipes

Burgers & Sandwiches

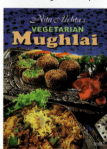

Vegetarian MUGHLAI

CHOCOLATE Cookbook

Indian Vegetarian Favourites

NITA MEHTA COOKERY CLUB

Become a MEMBER

Get FREE Cookooks

Register at : www.nitamehta.com

Now you can buy Nita Mehta & Tanya Mehta books with your credit card

Buy Online at www.nitamehta.com